T0017363

NOOSHE JAAN!

Bon appetit! نوش جان

THE ABCs OF PERSIAN FOOD

written by
Sunny Sanaz Shokrae

illustrated by
Ly Ngo Heisig

Abrams Appleseed • New York

A

is for

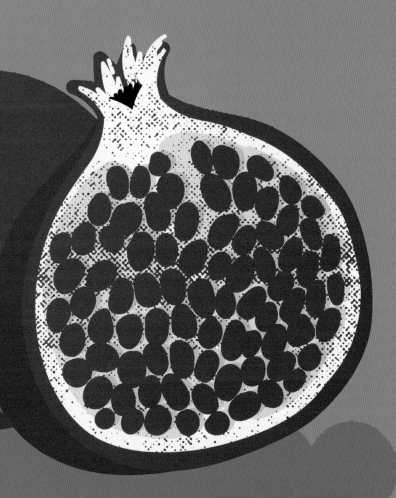

Anar
انار

B

is for

Baghali pokhte

باقالی پخته

C

is for

Cha'i
چای

D
is for

Doogh
دوغ

E

is for

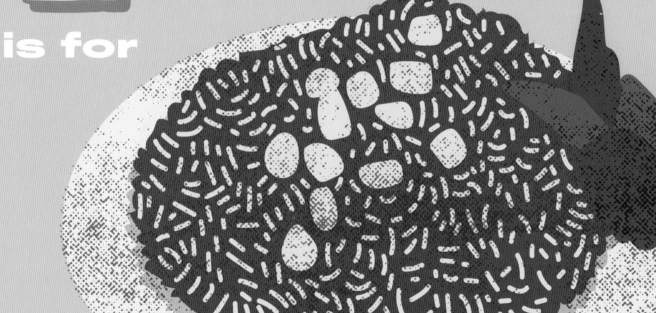

Estamboli polo
استانبولی پلو

F is for

Fesenjān

فسنجان

G

is for

Golāb
گلاب

H
is for

Haft-Sin

هفت‌سین

I

is for

Iranian pizza

پیتزای ایرانی

J is for

Joojeh kabob
جوجه کباب

K

is for

Khoresh karafs

خورش کرفس

L is for

Lavashak
لواشک

M

is for

Mast-o-khiyar

ماست و خیار

N
is for

Nân-e sangak
نان سنگک

O

is for

Olivieh

الویه

P

is for

Pesteh

پسته

Q

is for

Qottab

قطاب

R is for

Reshteh polo

رشته پلو

S

is for

Sabzi khordan
سبزی خوردن

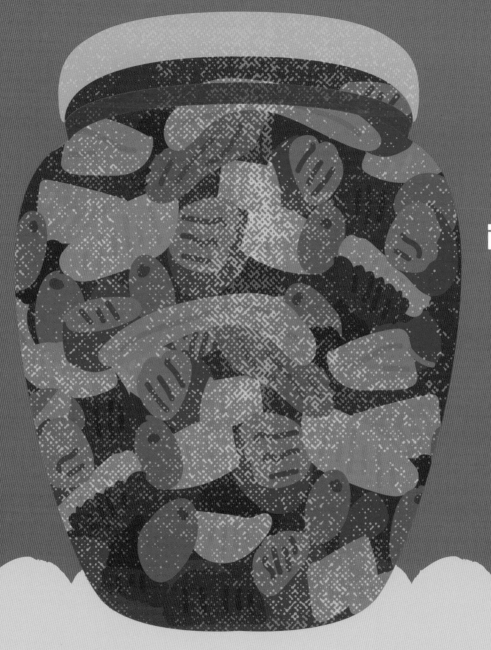

T

is for

Torshi

ترشی

U

is for

Kuku
كوكو

V is for

Valak polo
والک پلو

W

is for

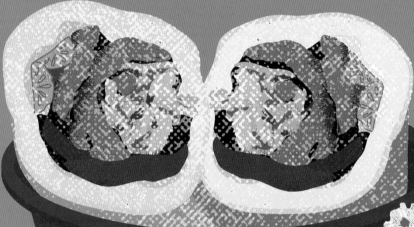

Westwood takeout

وستوود بیرون بر

X

is for

Xtra crispy tadiq

ته‌دیگ اکسترا کریسپی

Y

is for

Yakh dar behesht

یخ در بهشت

Z

is for

Zereshk
زرشک

That looks *delicious!* What's in it?

Anar
نار
ah-NAHR

The pomegranate is Iran's national fruit, symbolizing abundance, fertility, rebirth, and life. The juicy, ruby-red seeds are used in many dishes all year—but especially during the Winter Equinox/the Yalda holiday, which takes place during the longest and darkest night of the year.

Baghali pokhte
باقالی پخته
bah-ghal-lee
POKH-teh

Cooked fava beans, one of the most popular snacks in winter and spring served with salt, vinegar, and golpar spice. Just pop them out of their pods and into your mouth!

Cha'i
چای
chah-ee

Persian tea, made with loose leaf black tea, comes in a variety of subtle flavors, but is always a deep reddish-brown color. It is served with nabat (crystalized sugar candy) or a sugar cube. For most Persians, the day starts with a cup of tea, ends with a cup of tea, and in between meals there are even more cups of tea!

Doogh
دوغ
DOOG

A refreshing, fizzy, savory yogurt-based drink, served chilled. The perfect beverage to drink with any rich Persian meal.

Estamboli polo
استانبولی پلو
ess-TAM-boh-lee
PO-loh

A combination of rice, diced tomatoes, tomato paste, potatoes, and fried onions, this is one of the easiest Persian rice dishes to make. The name for this dish, sometimes spelled "estanboli," comes from the word "Istanbul," suggesting the influence of Turkish cuisine on this specific dish.

Fesenjān
فسنجان
feh-sehn-JHAN

Slow-cooked chicken stew with toasted walnuts and pomegranate molasses.

Golāb
گلاب
ghoh-LAHB

Rose water is an ingredient in many Persian desserts, jams, and ice creams. Since ancient times, it has also been used in medicine and perfume, and is served during celebrations and times of mourning for its calming effect.

Haft-Sin
هفت‌سین
hahft-SEEN

An arrangement of seven symbolic items for the Spring Equinox/Nowruz table, which is on display for the two-week-long New Year's celebrations beginning on March 20. Said to usher in prosperity, health, and good fortune for the New Year, the haft-sin, which translates to "the seven Ss," includes: seer (garlic), seeb (apple), samanu (wheat paste pudding), senjed (dried oleaster fruit), somagh (sumac), serkeh (vinegar), and sabzeh (sprouts).

Iranian pizza
پیتزای ایرانی
ih-RAH-nee-an PEET-za

A fast food favorite in Iran, piled with toppings that usually include a mixture of different types of meats, sausages, and cold cuts. It's common to dip your slice in ketchup, too!

Joojeh kabob
جوجه کباب
joo-JEH ka-BOB

Grilled chicken kabobs that are smothered in marinade with deep flavors of saffron and lemon.

Khoresh karafs
خورش کرفس
khor-ESH kar-AFS

Celery stew with sweet flavors of caramelized onions and a green broth tarted up with freshly squeezed lime and lemon.

Lavashak
لواشک
LAWV-oh-shack

A favorite snack for kids, this sour fruit leather is usually made at home by grandmothers who dry it in the sun on their rooftops during the summer months in Iran.

Mast-o-khiyar
ماست و خیار
MAH-sto KHEY-ar

A scrumptious Persian cucumber and yogurt mixture infused with herbs and served as a side dish.

Nân-e sangak
نان سنگک
nahn-EH
sahn-GAHK

Leavened flatbread baked on a bed of small river stones. This special bread is used to wrap around lamb kabobs, feta cheese and herbs, or enjoyed with stews such as dizi and abgoosht.

Olivieh
الویه
oh-LEE-vee-eh

This unique Persian potato salad is made with eggs, dill pickles, and chicken. (Recipes sometimes call for adding carrots and peas, too.) It is served as a perfect lunch or delightful appetizer.

Pesteh
پسته
peh-STEH

Pistachios are one of the most important crops grown in Iran. Persian pistachios are known for their quality and rich, unrivaled taste.

Qottab
قطاب
GHOH-tahb

A traditional Iranian almond-and-walnut-filled crescent pastry that is infused with cardamon and cinnamon, originally from the city of Yazd.

Reshteh polo
رشته پلو
rehsh-TEH POHL-oh

A fragrant rice and noodle dish often served during the New Year/Nowruz/Spring Equinox. The noodles symbolize the many winding paths we will choose from in the upcoming New Year.

Sabzi khordan
سبزی خوردن
sahb-ZEE
khohr-DAHN

A combination of herbs (such as spearmint, basil, flat leaf parsley, tarragon, dill, chives, and marjoram) often eaten with feta cheese, walnuts, radishes, scallions, and flatbread as a delicious breakfast or as a side dish with larger meals.

Torshi
ترشی
TOHR-shee

Pickled vegetables served on the side to act as a digestive aid, palate cleanser, and to balance rich meats and spices. Usually includes cauliflower, celery ribs, carrots, and cucumbers with cumin, coriander, cinnamon, and fennel.

Kuku
کوکو
KOO-koo

A Persian herb frittata made with eggs and a blend of chopped Persian herbs such as dill, parsley, and cilantro, plus spring onions and walnuts.

Valak polo
والک پلو
vah-LAHK POHL-oh

Valak, also known as wild garlic, is an herb that grows in the cool mountainous regions of Iran in the springtime. It is sweeter than typical garlic and is used to prepare fish, chicken, or meat dishes served with rice (polo).

Westwood takeout
وستوود بیرون بر
WEST-wud TAYK-out

The city of Los Angeles has the largest concentration of Iranian Americans in the United States. The L.A. neighborhood of Westwood in particular has become a thriving Persian community with specialty bakeries, restaurants, and stores. If you feel nostalgic for Iran, just visit Westwood for delicious takeout (known as "biroon-bar" in Persian) from one of its many amazing Iranian restaurants!

Xtra crispy tadiq
تهدیگ اکسترا کریسپی
EKS-trah KRIS-pee tah-DEEK

Tadiq is what Iranians call the crispy, delicious layer of golden-brown food that forms in the bottom of the pot while the food is cooking. It can be thinly sliced potatoes, rice mixed with yogurt, or flatbread that is left to crisp to perfection under a pile of steaming rice. Just be careful not to burn the tadiq!

Yahk dar behesht
یخ در بهشت
YAKH dahr beh-HESHT

"Ice in Paradise" is an elegant dessert made in the summertime with simple ingredients including milk, sugar, and rose water. It's delicate, aromatic, and served chilled.

Zereshk
زرشک
zehr-ESHK

Dried barberries are a tart and tangy ingredient used often in Persian cooking. They can be added to rice dishes to add little bursts of tartness to each bite. They can also be added to chicken dishes and egg-based dishes like kuku.

Author's Note

After becoming a mother, I couldn't find enough resources that celebrated my Iranian background in simple yet clever ways. As someone who speaks Persian but never learned to read or write the script, creating this book gave me something I could share with my young son to teach him not only about some of our favorite foods, but also how to pronounce their names, and how those names are written in Persian. Perhaps it was my upbringing as an Iranian in America, a California girl in New York, a perpetual outsider with one foot in each culture that inspired my attempt to bridge all the gaps I experienced growing up.

The ABCs of Persian Food is intended to support phonetics and teach the Persian language conversationally before a child can read or write. My hope is that it will serve as a tool for parents, caregivers, and teachers; bring joy to Persian food lovers or those with no Iranian background at all; and also build confidence in kids who take their Persian food to school. Perhaps after reading this book, they will open their lunchboxes and confidently boast about what's inside!

Nooshe jaan!

—Sunny Sanaz Shokrae

To listen to the author pronounce the words in this book, please visit abramsbooks.com/theabcsofpersianfood.

To Leo Arya, my little moosh, and to all the extraordinary 3rd culture kids who have grown up forging their own definition of home, transcending physical boundaries, and finding solace within the boundless realms of the heart. Special thank you to Nourin Alsharif for her invaluable Persian proofreading.

—S.S.S.

To my children, Lola, Colette, and little baby B.B.—may you wander this earth in search of the extraordinary and stay wildly curious.

—L.N.H.

The artwork for this book was created digitally.

Cataloging-in-Publication Data has been applied for and may be obtained from the Library of Congress.

ISBN 978-1-4197-6855-2
Text © 2024 Sunny Sanaz Shokrae
Illustrations © 2024 Ly Ngo Heisig

Book design by Ly Ngo Heisig and Natalie Padberg Bartoo

Published in 2024 by Abrams Appleseed, an imprint of ABRAMS. All rights reserved. No portion of this book may be reproduced, stored in a retrieval system, or transmitted in any form or by any means, mechanical, electronic, photocopying, recording, or otherwise, without written permission from the publisher.

Abrams Appleseed® is a registered trademark of Harry N. Abrams, Inc.

Printed and bound in China
10 9 8 7 6 5 4 3 2 1

For bulk discount inquiries, contact specialsales@abramsbooks.com.

ABRAMS The Art of Books
195 Broadway, New York, NY 10007
abramsbooks.com